Cryptocurrency

An Exploration Of The Historic, Current, And Future
Aspects Of Digital Currencies And Blockchain Technology
In The Crypto Revolution

*(Crypto Chronicles: A Comprehensive Tour Of The
Cryptocurrency Scene Examining Digital Currencies)*

Marcus Neuner

TABLE OF CONTENT

Diversifying Your Business

Your mining business will be your principal asset when you begin mining. By far, it's the most lucrative for you. The stakes are high when you rely on a single purchase. For instance, you run the risk of losing money on your mining equipment if the cryptocurrency you're mining goes through a prolonged decline.

It would help if you began withdrawing funds regularly when your mining business is performing well due to this and numerous other possible risks to your firm. Then, you should invest some of the money you make in mining into other ventures. Mining different cryptocurrencies is one approach to this. Staying with the market leaders is a good idea, but remember to keep an eye out for prospective initial coin offerings (ICOs). With some of the money you earn from your initial mining activities, you can invest in mining equipment for different cryptocurrencies. You have a higher chance of weathering market storms if you spread your investments out.

With the money you earn mining, diversify into other cryptocurrencies, and think about investing in different kinds of enterprises. You could launch a physical storefront with the money you make from your online venture. To further shorten the learning curve of operating your current firm, it is ideal to construct something compatible with it. A computer sales and repair store could be a good fit for you if, for instance, you have extensive expertise in building, fixing, and optimizing your mining rig. You might also get the tools you need to fix your mining gear from your own company. Ultimately, it is your decision. You also have the option of establishing a wholly distinct enterprise from your cryptocurrency mining operation if you so desire.

If you own cryptocurrency, when is the best time to sell it?

As you mine more and more cryptocurrency, you're probably asking when it's the right time to sell. The ever-changing Bitcoin market poses this problem to all miners on a constant basis.

Knowing the three steps of selling cryptocurrency might make the process much easier for you. Nobody owns a mining enterprise with the luxury of sitting on their hands and waiting for the market to go up before selling. The most effective strategy for this is to think about why you are selling.

• Cleaning Up After Operations

Maintaining financial stability for your company is the primary goal of the initial sales phase. You should be able to put food on the table and meet your expenses with your business activities. To cover these expenses, you'll have to convert some cryptocurrency into fiat currency. To keep the mining operations running, you'll need this.

A company's operational and maintenance expenses can eat up to 80% of its income for some. Simply exchanging a small amount of your cryptocurrency holdings will cover these expenses. For instance, you can trade in coins worth about $200 if your power bill is $200.

In addition to paying the power bill, you'll have to take money out of your account to maintain a healthy emergency fund. You should set aside 20-100% of your rig's value as a rainy-day fund as you're accumulating your capital. As an example, if the parts for your equipment are $1,000, you should set aside $200 to $1,000 for emergencies. When a component in your rig breaks, you can use this quantity.

It would be best if you immediately reloaded your emergency savings after spending from it. The selling phase, which includes operations maintenance, will also encompass this. For this aim, selling cryptocurrency once a month is ideal.

You should sell when the market is experiencing a brief uptrend when engaging in this kind of selling. When examining the price chart, bide your time until the market reaches a 5- or 10-day high, at which point you should sell enough cryptocurrency to cover your costs.

• Making a profit

You may occasionally notice an uptick in the cryptocurrency you are holding. Even though the market is unstable, there are moments when the value increases by 10% to 20%. It is advisable to sell a cryptocurrency if its value rises by 15% within a month while you still have it. We refer to this as a profit-taking sale. You take advantage of the opportunity to profit rather than feeling compelled to spend the money on something.

- Long-Term Employment

The long-term position is the final category of bitcoin sales. In the bitcoin market, this is what the majority of individuals are doing. When a cryptocurrency's market price drops, they buy, and when it rises again, they start selling. A trade that lasts for months or years would be considered a long-term position if it were the stock market.

Things move considerably more quickly in the Bitcoin market. Typically, a long-term job lasts a few weeks. There hasn't been a Bitcoin rise lasting longer than two weeks since the end of 2017. There can be, nevertheless, longer-term investments in emerging cryptocurrencies. As of right now, Bitcoin has just recovered from its all-time high at the start of the year. It is entirely feasible for a different cryptocurrency to achieve significant milestones.

Keeping Knowledgeable and Current

Making lucrative selections also requires keeping up with current events and trends. Given the dynamic nature of the digital ecosystem, Gen Z investors must take proactive measures to obtain dependable and precise information in order to traverse the intricacies of cryptocurrency markets effectively. This subsection will examine the significance of employing Bitcoin news outlets and offer insightful advice on how to get the most out of them.

Crypto news sources are websites that compile and disseminate information on the cryptocurrency market, including news, commentary, and expert viewpoints. Websites, blogs, podcasts, social media profiles, and even conventional media outlets that cover cryptocurrency-related subjects might be considered as these sources. Effective use of these resources can provide Gen Z investors with a competitive advantage and help them make wise decisions.

Being able to keep up with market trends, price swings, and regulatory developments is one of the main advantages of Bitcoin news sources. Effective risk management and the identification of possible investment opportunities depend on timely and accurate information. Gen Z investors can learn about impending initial coin offerings (ICOs), new cryptocurrencies, and technological developments that may have an impact on the market by subscribing to credible news sources.

Also, news outlets covering cryptocurrencies can offer insightful commentary from professionals in the field. Gen Z investors can learn from the accomplishments and errors of more seasoned traders, analysts, and investors by reading or watching interviews with them. These professional judgments can provide guidance for investment plans, point out possible hazards, and present different viewpoints on the market.

But it's crucial to keep in mind the reliability and standing of the news sources. Given the proliferation of false information and fake news, Gen Z investors need to confirm the integrity of the information they are given. The credibility of the report can be increased by examining the source's reputation, cross-referencing data from other sources, and depending on reputable outlets.

Gen Z investors should think about diversifying their sources in order to make the most out of their cryptocurrency news sources. Diverse platforms may offer distinct viewpoints and views, facilitating a comprehensive comprehension of the market. Talking with members of the cryptocurrency community on social media or in forums can also yield up-to-date information on market movements.

For Gen Z investors in the Bitcoin space, being up to date on the most recent developments is crucial. In the constantly changing world of cryptocurrencies, young investors can boost their chances of success and make successful judgments by learning from industry professionals, using reliable news sources, and keeping up with market trends.

Order placement on Binance: One of the critical components of trading cryptocurrencies is placing orders on Binance. To purchase or sell cryptocurrencies on its platform, traders can choose from a variety of charges offered by Binance. Every kind of order has a distinct function and helps traders carry out their trading plans effectively. The following describes some typical order types on Binance:

1. Market Order: The most basic kind of order is a market order. You are giving Binance instructions to purchase or sell a cryptocurrency at the going rate when you submit a market order. Market

orders are filled fast, but because of price volatility, the precise price at which the order is filled may differ significantly from the going rate. Market orders are appropriate for traders who are less concerned with the accurate price and want to make a trade right away.

2. Limit Order: Using a limit order, you can be very specific about the price you wish to pay for or receive when buying or selling cryptocurrencies. A buy-limit order will only be filled if the market price hits or falls below the price you have selected. A sell limit order will only be filled if the market price hits or exceeds the price you have chosen. Limit orders provide you greater control over the price at which they are executed, but they might only be filled if the market meets your desired price.

5. OCO (One Cancels the Other) Order: An OCO order lets you place a take-profit and a stop-loss order at the same time.

The other charge is immediately canceled if one of these is carried out. This risk management tool aids traders in limiting losses or locking in winnings.

6. Trailing Stop Order: This type of order is a dynamic stop-loss order that is modified in response to changes in the price of the cryptocurrency. The stop price tracks the market price at a predetermined distance, and you can select a trailing percentage or a fixed amount. The stop price moves with the market if it swings in your favor, assisting you in protecting your winnings. The stop price stays set until it is reached, even in the event of a market reversal.

7. Iceberg Order: An order placed via an iceberg order conceals a sizable order from the order book. To keep other traders from knowing about your trading intentions, only a piece of the order is revealed. More of the order becomes apparent when the visible part is completed until the entire order is filled.

It's critical to take your trading strategy, risk tolerance, and market conditions into account while placing orders on Binance. Your unique objectives will determine the order type you choose, including whether you want to execute rapidly, set price thresholds, or use risk management techniques. Additionally, before confirming, carefully review the terms of your order because mistakes can have unanticipated consequences for your trades.

Selecting an exchange for cryptocurrencies.

After creating your Bitcoin wallet, the next step to begin trading cryptocurrencies is to choose a reliable cryptocurrency exchange. Online markets where you may purchase, sell, and even trade various cryptocurrencykinds are known as cryptocurrency exchanges.

Safety: Security has to be the first consideration when selecting a business. Discussions must also follow legal criteria.

Credibility and Reputation: Analyze user reviews and the reputation of the exchange. A safe trading environment is more likely to be provided by a respectable business with a solid reputation.

Digital Money Encouraged: Check to see if the exchange accepts the coins you wish to trade. Although some businesses focus on specific markets, others provide a more extensive range.

In favor of Fiat Money: If you plan to buy cryptocurrencies with traditional fiat currencies like USD or EUR, choose an exchange that enables you to do so. Only some businesses provide fiat on-ramps.

Commissions are fees that exchange charges to execute trades. Compare an exchange's fee structures to those of other markets to find one that works for your trading style and budget.

Improved price execution and lower spreads could be the outcome of increased transaction volume and liquidity. Exchanges with higher liquidity offer a more seamless trading experience.

Please make sure the exchange's UI is intuitive and suitable for your trading style by taking a close look at it. Certain businesses are designed with inexperienced traders in mind, while others cater to seasoned investors.

Client support: Reliable customer assistance may be required if you encounter issues or have questions. Check the responsiveness of the exchange and its support channels before you start trading.

Types of Exchanges for Cryptocurrencies

Centralized exchanges (CEXs), which are managed by centralized entities, are the most often used type of exchanges. They offer a wide range of cryptocurrencies, excellent liquidity, and intuitive user interfaces. Among the instances are Coinbase, Binance, and Kraken.

Decentralized exchanges, or DEXs, function without a central authority and allow users to perform transactions straight from their wallets. Even if they offer more control and privacy, they could have less liquidity. Popular DEXs include Uniswap and SushiSwap.

Peer-to-Peer (P2P) Communications: P2P exchanges facilitate direct transactions between buyers and sellers, eliminating the need for an intermediary. They often accept many payment modes and are prevalent in areas where regular banking is not easily accessible.

Make extensive research

Before you start trading on an exchange, do a lot of research. Examine the exchange's past security incidents, review user feedback, and make sure it conforms with all relevant laws and regulations. Furthermore, consider starting with a small test transaction to see how the exchange functions and how easy it is to use.

An essential initial step is to decide which option best suits your demands for trading cryptocurrencies. Because it can significantly affect your trading style, take your time choosing one that aligns with your goals and preferences. In the following chapters of this course, we'll look at creating an account on a cryptocurrency exchange, completing your first transaction, and developing effective trading strategies.

Creating an Account on a Crypto Exchange

The procedure for creating an account typically includes the following steps:

To finish the registration process, go to the exchange's website and click the "Sign Up" or "Register" option. It will be necessary to provide your

Verification: In order to comply with Know Your Customer (KYC) and Anti-Money Laundering (AML) regulations, exchanges frequently require identity verification. This requires you to provide personal information, such as your full name, birthdate, and often a scan of a passport or government-issued ID. Pay close attention to the exchange's instructions

Section I

What is volatility in the market?

A key idea in finance, market volatility describes how much the prices of financial assets fluctuate over a given time frame. It's a reflection of how financial markets are dynamic and constantly evolving. When assessing the risk of different financial assets, volatility is a critical component that influences investing choices.Statistical tools are commonly used to measure volatility, and the standard deviation is one widely used method. This statistical metric aids in estimating the degree to which the price of an asset deviates from its average over a given period. Increased volatility translates into more significant price swings, which suggests increased risk.Market volatility can be attributed to multiple sources. Economic events like shifts in interest rates or other economic indicators can bring on volatility. Political occurrences like elections or modifications to governmental regulations may have a significant effect on market stability.Another essential factor influencing volatility is market sentiment. When it comes to asset prices, good news might cause a purchasing frenzy, while bad news can cause a sell-off. The way investors respond to information and how they feel about things can either increase or decrease market volatility.Financial instruments vary in terms of volatility as well. For example, because stocks have a higher risk-return profile than bonds, they are typically more volatile. Extreme volatility can be seen in commodities and cryptocurrencies due to speculative trading and dynamics of supply and demand.Volatility is actively dealt with by market participants, such as hedge funds, retail traders, and institutional investors. While some trading techniques try to reduce risk by hedging against volatility, others strive to profit from short-term market swings.Central banks and government policies, such as interest rate adjustments, quantitative easing, or regulatory changes can also influence the volatility of the market. Financial markets may be stabilized or destabilized by these operations.

Now let's look at some more instances of market volatility:

1. Stock Market Volatility: One of the best examples of a daily environment

with volatility is the stock market. Significant price fluctuations in individual stocks might occur in response to news about competitors in the industry, corporate earnings reports, or world economic events. For example, during the global stock market crisis of 2008, there was tremendous volatility, resulting in the rapid loss of value of numerous stocks.

2. Cryptocurrency Volatility: Extreme price volatility is a well-known characteristic of cryptocurrencies such as Ethereum and Bitcoin. In a matter of hours or days, these digital assets may see abrupt price increases followed by precipitous drops. Variables like market sentiment, technological developments, and news about regulations significantly influence prices for cryptocurrencies.

3. Volatility of the Commodities Market: There is volatility associated with commodities such as gold, oil, and agricultural items. Weather-related variables, geopolitical conflicts, and mismatches in supply and demand can

cause significant price changes. For instance, disruptions in the collection of oil from large producers may result in a spike in oil prices that impacts economies and markets throughout the world.

4. Foreign Exchange (Forex) Market Volatility: Interest rate fluctuations, the release of economic data,

5. Bond Market Volatility: Bonds are subject to volatility even though they are typically regarded as safer investments than equities. Changes in interest rates, downgrades in credit ratings, and mood swings in the market can all affect the price of bonds. For example, bond prices may decline in response to central banks' unexpected announcements of interest rate hikes, creating volatility in the bond market.

6. The VIX, or Volatility Index: Known as the "fear gauge," the VIX gauges anticipated volatility in the stock market. When investors expect more market volatility, it rises. The VIX typically

spikes during times of geopolitical unrest or economic uncertainty, indicating growing market anxieties. These instances show how a variety of assets and marketplaces, each impacted by particular causes, can be affected by market volatility. To control and even profit from this volatility, traders and investors employ a variety of tactics, including diversification and options trading. In order to preserve stability and shield investors from sharp market fluctuations, financial institutions and regulators also keep a careful eye on market volatility.

3 Cryptocurrency Money Laundering

This is, for the most part, the most prevalent type of financial crime in the cryptocurrency industry. Despite the fact that the exchanges offer a KYC procedure, there are a number of exclusions that help the criminals transfer the money.

When it comes to cryptocurrencies, this can entail thieves turning money they've gained illegally into cryptocurrency and then utilizing that money to buy products and services.

It might be challenging to follow these transactions because cryptocurrencies are decentralized and not subject to financial institution or governmental regulation.

3.1 Offenses that Precede

Typical money laundering methods are often the result of predicate offenses such as drug trafficking, fraud, and corruption. One of the most common base charges in cryptocurrency money laundering is cybercrime. Cybercriminals who commit crimes like phishing and hacking can make substantial profits in cryptocurrencies. After that, they launder their illegal gains using these monies.

For instance, a hacker might get into a victim's exchange account or bitcoin wallet and take their cryptocurrency assets. After then, the hacker has two options: either sell the bitcoin they took on an internet exchange or spend the money to buy more. The hacker can "clean" the stolen money this way, making it harder to find them.

Ransomware attacks are another prevalent type of cybercrime that can result in the money laundering of cryptocurrency. The perpetrator of a ransomware attack encrypts the victim's data and requests payment in cryptocurrency in return for the key to recover it. The ransom is paid by the victim in bitcoin, which the perpetrator then launders.

After being laundered through bitcoin transactions, the money can be used to finance new illegal operations or to buy legal things without raising any red flags.

3.2 The Three Phases of Laundering Cryptocurrency

Money laundering with cryptocurrency poses a severe problem for law enforcement and is a developing worry. Many governments and regulatory organizations are drafting new laws and rules to strengthen traceability and transparency in the bitcoin market in order to address this problem.

3.2.1 Arrangement

The process by which the proceeds of illicit activity are "placed" into the financial system is known as the placement stage of money laundering. When it comes to cryptocurrencies, this may entail taking the money obtained by illegal activity, turning it into a cryptocurrency like Bitcoin, and then sending it to a private online wallet.

One instance of cryptocurrency money laundering could be a criminal who accepts cash payment for selling stolen items. The perpetrator may then use the money to purchase cryptocurrencies on an authorized exchange, hiding the source of the funds and making it more difficult for law enforcement to find them. By doing this, the money would be introduced into the financial system in a way that would be challenging to track down and enable the criminal to start layering the money to hide its origins further.

By doing this, the money would be brought into the financial system without creating a visible trace of its source. The money launderer might then employ a variety of techniques, like transferring the money to several wallets or trading it for other cryptocurrencies, to layer the funds and make it harder to track them down.

After the money is in the virtual wallet, the fraudster can move it to another wallet or use it to buy products or services. Because the transactions are made using cryptocurrencies, which are decentralized and not governed by the same laws as conventional financial institutions, it may be challenging for law authorities to track down the money.

There are two typical ways to arrange cryptocurrency.

Comprehending Blockchain Technology

Blockchain: What Is It?

Although blockchain is a ground-breaking technology that powers digital currencies like Bitcoin, its applications go well beyond this. Fundamentally, a blockchain is an open, transparent, decentralized ledger that tracks and validates transactions via a network of computers.

A list of transactions is contained in each block that makes up a blockchain. Any information that can be digitally stored, including ownership records and digital assets, can be transferred through these transactions. As a result of the blocks' chronological connections to one another, a chain is formed; hence, the term "blockchain."

The decentralized nature of blockchain technology is its distinguishing feature. A distributed network of users known as nodes maintains and verifies a blockchain, in contrast to conventional centralized systems where a single authority controls the ledger. To guarantee agreement on the ledger's current state, every node independently verifies the transactions and maintains a copy of the complete blockchain.

Hash functions are used to cryptographically protect transactions, which are bundled together into blocks to maintain the blockchain's security and integrity. Hash functions transform the data in a block into a fixed-length character string called a hash. These distinct hashes serve as the data's digital fingerprints. Any alteration to the data, regardless of size, will produce a totally new hash and notify the network of any attempted manipulation.

Every block also carries a reference to the hash of the previous block, which functions as a connection between them. This connecting mechanism guarantees the blockchain's immutability. A block's hash must be changed for it to be removed or altered, which makes it very difficult to do so after it is put to the chain and for all blocks that come after. Due to the ability to audit and validate the complete transaction history, this feature fosters confidence and transparency.

Transparency is another critical component of blockchain technology. The blockchain, being a distributed ledger, enables all users to access and verify the transactions recorded on the network. Participants' trust is increased by this transparency, which also lessens the need for intermediaries or outside verification.

Blockchain technology was first created for cryptocurrencies, but it is now recognized for its potential uses in many other industries. Blockchain offers the ability to facilitate safe and effective data transfers without the need for intermediaries, which might simplify procedures, lower fraud, and boost confidence across a wide range of industries.

Gaining an understanding of the foundations of blockchain technology is crucial for comprehending the possible advantages and difficulties linked to cryptocurrencies, as well as for investigating the broader uses of this revolutionary technology in the following chapters.

The Dynamics of Reversals in the Market

Understanding the factors driving price fluctuations is crucial for reversal trading success. The undercurrents that can move prices in unanticipated directions are produced by these factors, often known as market dynamics.

We will examine these dynamics and their role in market reversals in this chapter.

Unbalances and Reversals in Supply and Demand

It's essential to comprehend supply and demand in order to trade FX. The exchanges between suppliers and purchasers set market prices. Thus, when supply and demand are out of balance, reversals happen.

Let's examine how these imbalances cause price reversals.

Bearish Reversal: Supply Growing and Demand Falling

Imagine that the market is experiencing an upward trend. The 'demand' side of the equation, or buyers, is in charge and is driving up prices by acquiring the asset. On the other hand, a number of variables may cause supply to rise while demand falls:

Overvaluation: If prices keep going up, buyers can begin to feel that the asset is too expensive. This attitude lessens their propensity to purchase, which lowers demand.

Profit Objectives: Certain purchasers might have attained their intended profit objectives and choose to liquidate their holdings in order to secure their profits.

By doing this, the market's supply is increased.

Profit Protection: Early market entrants who have unrealized profits may choose to liquidate their holdings in order to safeguard their gains. Additionally, this operation raises the supply.

Simultaneously, sellers perceive a chance to sell at high prices, so augmenting the market's supply. An rise in store and a reduction in demand may result in a bearish reversal.

Reversal in the Bull Market: Falling Supply and Rising Demand

On the other hand, the market is experiencing a downward trend. The'supply' side, or sellers, are in control. Prices are falling as they offload the asset.

But as long as prices continue to decline, sellers begin to liquidate their holdings. This can be the result of their wanting to reduce their losses or because they've hit their earnings goals. As a result, there needs to be more supply on the market. Meanwhile, purchasers begin to perceive an opening. Their initial purchase seems alluring due to the low price, which raises market demand.

The current situation is one of rising demand and falling supply.

Identifying the Phase of Consolidation

Price frequently goes through a consolidation phase, moving sideways within a small range, prior to a reversal. This stage can reveal information regarding the future direction of prices:

Indecision: The market is still determining during the consolidation phase. The goal of both buyers and sellers is to take the reins. This stage frequently comes before an imbalance in supply and demand and a possible reversal in price.

Breakout Point: The direction of the reversal may be shown by a breakout from the consolidation range. A bullish reversal is indicated by a breakout above the field and a bearish one by a flight below.

Volume Analysis: Volume typically rises at the breakout point and falls during the consolidation stage. This pattern can further confirm the direction of the reversal.

An illustration of a consolidation phase with lower volume and an upside breakout on rising volume

Recall that understanding supply and demand is a skill that takes time and experience to master. You can become more adept at spotting possible market reversals by taking these things into account.

Skills and Education: Although having a basic understanding of cryptocurrencies is vital, it's also critical to build the skills and obtain the education required to succeed in this quickly changing industry. We'll go over the abilities you'll need and how to further your cryptocurrency education here:

Constant Learning: The world of cryptocurrency is dynamic and constantly evolving. It's imperative to keep up with the most recent news, trends, and advancements.

Technical Analysis: Knowing technical analysis is essential for anyone interested in trading or investing in cryptocurrency. This entails examining price charts, spotting trends, and utilizing a range of indicators to help you decide. You can gauge market mood and improve the accuracy of your price movement forecasts by using technical analysis.

Security Procedures: In the world of cryptocurrencies, security is crucial. Discover how to defend your digital assets from efforts at theft and hacking. Enable two-factor authentication (2FA), create solid and one-of-a-kind passwords, and think about utilizing hardware wallets for long-term storage. Watch out for frauds and phishing attempts.

Risk management: The prices of cryptocurrencies can swing significantly, and the markets are notoriously volatile. Create a risk management plan that involves limiting your investments to what you can afford to lose, diversifying your holdings, and placing stop-loss orders. Achieving a balance between your comfort level of risk and the potential benefits is crucial.

Comprehending Market attitude: News, social media, and philosophy all frequently impact cryptocurrency markets. Making better trading judgments can be aided by developing your ability to assess market sentiment. Watch news sources, forums, and social media sites for indications of changes in market mood.

Tax Awareness: Depending on the tax laws in your nation, cryptocurrency transactions may have an impact on your taxes. To guarantee that tax regulations are followed, get advice from a tax expert with experience in bitcoin.

Regulatory Expertise: Keep yourself updated about the laws and regulations in your nation. Different jurisdictions may have quite other legislation regarding cryptocurrencies. Staying informed about legal requirements and possible updates will assist you in avoiding legal problems.

Technical Skills: If you're interested in developing blockchain applications or starting your cryptocurrency venture, you should study programming languages that are frequently used in the blockchain industry. Examples of these languages are Solidity, which is used for Ethereum-based smart contracts, and Python and JavaScript, which are used for blockchain development.

Networking: Making contacts within the bitcoin community has several advantages. Join like-minded people in cryptocurrencymeetups, conferences, and online forums to exchange ideas, learn from others, and discuss possible partnerships.

Psychological Resilience: The volatility of cryptocurrency markets can be emotionally exhausting. Build psychological toughness to manage the strain brought on the market swings. Refrain from acting on impulse or out of greed or fear.

Ethical Awareness: Recognize the moral ramifications of your behavior in the bitcoin community. Following moral guidelines promotes trust and helps the industry flourish positively overall.

Entrepreneurial attitude: Develop an entrepreneurial mindset if you're thinking of starting a project or business involving cryptocurrencies. This covers abilities like strategic thinking, business planning, and market research.

By devoting time and energy to honing these abilities and advancing your knowledge in the realm of cryptocurrencies, you will increase your chances of success, reduce risks, and make well-informed judgments.

T

Even though these advancements were revolutionary, they also presented new difficulties. As centralized systems grew to be data powerhouses, worries about information monopolization, security, and privacy arose. Financial and informational transactions still primarily relied on intermediaries, such as banks, service providers, or platforms. Although the Digital Revolution made information more widely accessible, it did not always translate into more democratic governance.

This is the environment in which cryptocurrencies and blockchain technology developed. These technologies were envisioned as an alternative to centralized control, offering a peer-to-peer, transparent, and secure transaction environment free from the influence of a central authority. The ramifications were significant. Digital money, intelligent contracts, and unchangeable data are all possible. Blockchain was positioned to be the next big thing in the Digital Revolution, upending our fundamental ideas about authority, trust, and the transfer of wealth in the digital age.

We shall go more into the development of these technologies, their guiding ideas, and the revolutionary possibilities they offer for our globalized society in the ensuing chapters. 1.2. Goal of the Book

Differentiating fact from fiction in a world complete with information can be difficult, particularly in a topic as complex and fast-developing as blockchain and cryptocurrencies. The fundamental ideas and revolutionary possibilities of decentralized technology can quickly be eclipsed by the hype, disputes, and meteoric spikes and falls in

Bitcoin valuations. The noise makes it simple to become lost.

To cut through this noise, "Blockchain and Cryptocurrencies: Decoding the Digital Ledger" aims to clarify things. This book is meant to be a thorough reference for people from a variety of backgrounds, from the tech-savvy enthusiast looking to expand their knowledge to the total beginner wondering what the big deal is about.

Our goal is to Dispel the myths around blockchain technology and cryptocurrency.

Give a historical overview and describe the development of these technologies.

Examine practical uses and the possibility of societal influence.

Talk about typical misunderstandings and disputes.

Provide a forecast for the development of decentralized digital technologies.

Our goal is for readers to leave this journey with a comprehensive grasp of blockchain technology and cryptocurrencies, as well as the ability to participate in intelligent debates, make wise choices, and contribute to the continued development of this new frontier in technology. This book aims to empower its readers in the digital world, not only help them understand technology.

B. Recognizing the Blockchain's Necessity

Blockchain is essentially a distributed, decentralized ledger that keeps track of transactions across several nodes or computers. Blockchain uses cryptography to guarantee immutability, security, and transparency in contrast to traditional centralized systems.

The demand for blockchain technology is primarily driven by the need to address the problem of trust in digital transactions. Trust is created in many traditional systems by means of centralized intermediaries like governments, banks, or other third-party organizations. However, the lack of confidence and transparency in transactions might result from these intermediaries' susceptibility to manipulation, hacking, or corruption. Blockchain presents a substitute by offering a transparent and unchangeable mechanism in which network members establish trust by reaching a consensus.

Blockchain technology also solves the security and integrity of data issues. Data can be purposefully or inadvertently changed, removed, or manipulated in traditional databases. On the other hand, blockchain creates an irreversible history of all transactions by sequentially and immutably recording them. The data integrity is ensured by the fact that once a transaction is registered on the blockchain, it is very impossible to change or tamper with.

The ability of blockchain to facilitate peer-to-peer transactions without the need for intermediaries is another significant feature. Blockchain can lower transaction costs, expedite settlement times, and increase financial inclusion by doing away with intermediaries. This is especially important in areas where existing systems are frequently expensive and inefficient, like micropayments, remittances, and cross-border payments.

Supply chains can now be more accountable and transparent thanks to blockchaintechnology.which tracks the flow of commodities and verifies their validity. This supports ethical sourcing methods, lowers counterfeiting, and ensures the quality of the products.

Furthermore, blockchain can improve data control and privacy. People can use blockchain technology to selectively share their personal data, giving them more control over it than they would have with centralized organizations. This is especially important in the significant data era, when worries about data breaches and illegal access to personal data are shared.

It's crucial to remember, though, that blockchain technology is only sometimes a universally applicable answer. Scalability, energy consumption, and regulatory issues are some of its drawbacks. When implementing blockchain technologies, the particular use case and associated trade-offs must be carefully considered.

In conclusion, the demand for efficiency, security, trust, and transparency across a range of businesses is what drives the necessity for blockchain technology. It provides a tamper-proof, decentralized system that can tackle issues with data privacy, supply chain transparency, peer-to-peer transactions, trust, and data integrity. Blockchain has the power to revolutionize sectors and change how transactions are carried out, opening the door for a more secure and decentralized digital future even while it is not a cure-all.

Acquiring Access To A Mining Pool

Mining Pools' Value

While mining alone may seem intriguing, it's essential to know why joining a mining pool is usually a superior option—especially for newcomers like you. This is the reason it matters:

Mining Challenge:

The mining difficulty of cryptocurrency networks is constantly changed to maintain a constant rate of block creation. This implies that mining a block alone gets increasingly tricky as additional miners join the network. Large mining farms often have processing power advantages over solo miners. By combining your resources with others, you can increase your chances of earning rewards by joining a mining pool.

Regular Payouts:

Finding a block can take a lot of time while mining alone. Days, weeks, or even months may pass between profitable mining endeavors. A more consistent income is guaranteed by mining pools, which offer regular returns based on the quantity of mining power you give.

Reduced Equipment Needs: Independent mining necessitates the use of solid equipment and a substantial energy expenditure. By joining mining pools, you can participate with less capable equipment, which lowers your initial outlay and recurring expenses.

Diversification: varying cryptocurrencies have varying levels of complexity, profitability, and market fluctuations. By pooling your mining resources across several currencies, you can increase your chances of success in the volatile world of cryptocurrencies.

Support and Community: A built-in support system is frequently present in mining pools. The pool's community or support team is there to assist you if you run into technical difficulties or have any inquiries. This is really beneficial in the beginning.

The Operation of Mining Pools

Mining pools are considered by many to be the foundation of cryptocurrency mining, especially for smaller miners. Let's dissect how they function:

Combining Resources: You collaborate with other miners to pool your computing power when you join a mining pool. Working together improves the likelihood of resolving challenging riddles that are required for transaction verification and adding new blocks to the blockchain.

Consider miners to be employees of a gold mine. When searching for gold alone, they could take a very long period in one place. However, they can cover more land more effectively when they cooperate (in a mining pool). If one of them cracks a problem or finds gold, the team as a whole splits the prize. This is how it functions.

Allocation of Block Advantages: Members of the pool split up the benefits as they work together to mine new blocks, and this process is called "hash rate." Your share of the prize money increases as you contribute more.

Imagine it as a pie. The amount of processing power you contribute to the pool determines the size of your slice. When the pool mines a block successfully, you will receive 10% of the total pie if your contribution is 10% of the real power.

Mining Software: In order to connect your equipment to the servers of a mining pool, you must have specialized software. Your mining efforts will be coordinated with those of other miners in the pool, thanks to this program.

Imagine yourself in charge of an orchestra as a conductor. By ensuring that all of the instruments (mining equipment) play in unison, the conductor increases the likelihood of producing beautiful music (mine a block).

Shares and Difficulty Levels: To keep track of each person's unique contribution, pools use "shares." These shares are more accessible to obtain since they are less challenging to get than the network. You will receive more benefits from the pool the more claims you give.

Consider shares as individual puzzle parts. The pool splits the 1,000-piece jigsaw that the network may have into 100-piece parts. You will receive 10% of the more significant challenge's prize if you solve ten of these more minor riddles.

Payment Procedures: Different reward distribution options, including Pay-Per-Share (PPS), Proportional, and Pay-Per-Last-N-Shares (PPLNS), are provided by pools. Every technique has advantages, and some miners may find more success with it than others.

Consider various approaches to dividing a meal bill. PPS is comparable to having a flat fee for all users. Sharing the bill proportionately means dividing it according to what each person ordered. Thanking the person who invited everyone to supper is similar to PPLNS.

Despite lacking top-notch mining equipment, joining a mining pool is a team approach to bitcoin mining that offers a better possibility of regular revenues. We'll walk you through the process of selecting the ideal collection for your needs in the next section.

- Categories of Losses

Losses can appear in a variety of ways in the realm of cryptocurrencies, each with unique traits and ramifications.

To correctly manage your assets and negotiate the complexity of taxation, you must identify and comprehend the many forms of bitcoin losses.

The following are the main categories of losses to be mindful of:

1. Capital Losses: - When you swap or sell a cryptocurrency for less than you paid for it initially, you may suffer capital losses.

When you sell a cryptocurrency and lock in its dropped value, you may incur these losses.

- When it comes to taxes, capital losses are an essential area. You can lower your total tax obligation by offsetting capital losses against capital gains, depending on your jurisdiction.

2. Trading Losses: - For aggressive cryptocurrency traders, trading losses are not uncommon. They arise from the quick purchasing and selling of cryptocurrencies, frequently in reaction to market turbulence.

- Depending on whether the cryptocurrency has been sold or is still being held, trading losses may be realized or unrealized. Taxation and financial management need to keep track of these losses.

3. Investment Losses: When the value of a cryptocurrency you've owned for a long time drastically drops, you may incur investment losses. These losses can add up, particularly in times of market turbulence.

- Losses on your investments are frequently only realized once you choose to sell the coin. A strategic consideration is knowing when and how to recognize these losses.

4. Losses Connected to Security:

- Security-related losses stem from things like fraud, theft of private keys, and hacking. Cryptocurrencies that are lost or stolen as a result of security breaches are considered losses.

It can be difficult to recover losses connected to security, but it's crucial to appropriately record them for tax purposes and evaluate how they will affect your entire Bitcoin portfolio.

5. Opportunity Losses: - Opportunity losses are the results of making certain

decisions that cause you to miss out on possible gains, like not investing in a cryptocurrency that goes on to see significant growth. Even if opportunity losses are rarely realized in the conventional sense, they nevertheless emphasize how crucial timing and decision-making are in the Bitcoin market.

Comprehending the many kinds of losses that might arise in the cryptocurrency realm is essential for managing risks, making financial plans, and handling taxes.

It enables you to decide when to sell when to hold, and when to reduce risk with knowledge.

Furthermore, efficiently handling your tax obligations depends on your ability to distinguish between realized and unrealized losses.

Whether you're a trader, investor, or just interested in learning more about digital assets, having this knowledge can help you make sense of the ever-changing and dynamic world of bitcoin losses and investments.

Recognize the Risks Associated with Cryptocurrency Investing

Be well aware of the possible risks associated with investing in cryptocurrencies before making any deposits. Here are some points to remember:

The value of cryptocurrency is erratic. Cryptocurrency prices are prone to extreme fluctuations, and losing money quickly is a constant risk.

The asset class of cryptocurrency is new and unproven. The long-term viability of any specific cryptocurrency cannot be guaranteed.

In the cryptocurrency space, there are a lot of con artists

In summary

Although it is inherently risky, investing in cryptocurrencies has the potential to be very profitable.

Important lessons learned

Think about the technology, team, use case, market capitalization, price volatility, and long-term potential of a cryptocurrency before investing.

Before making any cryptocurrency investments, conduct research.

Recognize the dangers of investing in cryptocurrencies, such as scams and volatility.

Case Study: An Effective Cryptocurrency Investment That Is Not Typical

Let's examine a case study of a profitable Bitcoin investment.

In 2011, a young investor named John bought 100 Bitcoins for $0.30 each. At the time, Bitcoin was a relatively unknown cryptocurrency with a minimal market capitalization. John was ready to risk his thirty dollars, though, because he thought Bitcoin had a lot of potential, and he felt he could afford to lose the money if it didn't work out.

Let's go back to the present day. At the time of writing,

This is just one example of how a successful cryptocurrency investment can be advantageous. However, it is essential to remember that cryptocurrency is a highly volatile asset without guaranteeing a successful outcome.

The Future of Cryptocurrency

The future of cryptocurrency is uncertain, but it is clear that this technology has the potential to change the world of finance. Cryptocurrencies could revolutionize the way we pay for goods and services, the way we invest our money, and the way we interact with the world around us.

Only time will tell what the future holds for cryptocurrency, but it is an exciting time to be involved in this space. If you are considering investing in cryptocurrency, do proper research and only invest money that you can afford to lose.

You already know a fair amount about cryptocurrency at this point. Through a process called mining, cryptocurrencies come into being. There are two parts to the operation of mining new coins. These are introducing new money into the system and adding transactions to the blockchain.

Cryptocurrency mining

It would help if you had specialized software and a powerful computer to mine cryptocurrencies. Modern, high-tech machines designed especially for mining cryptocurrencies are available on the market.

Anyone who dedicates their time to verifying cryptocurrency transactions and adding new currencies to the network is referred to as a miner. Cryptocurrency mining demands a lot of resources. This method requires expensive computers, and running costs are very high. This is due to the high electrical consumption of the mining operation.

Generally speaking, miners spend most of their time attempting to use hash algorithms to verify a block containing data. It's critical first to comprehend the foundational ideas behind blockchain technology in order to understand better how the mining process operates.

Blockchain Technology and Mining

The blockchain is a type of publicly distributed, decentralized ledger used by cryptocurrencies. The mining procedure plays a part in making blockchain safe networks. As a result, mining is a crucial part of the blockchain and is vital to its stability. Because every transaction on the blockchain is validated by the process, it adds an extra degree of security.

In actuality, the blockchain ensures the legitimacy of every Bitcoin token. A hash pointer is something that is present in every block. Since there is no single server to record every transaction, the blockchain is decentralized. However, the blockchain ledger can only function with enough processing power. The combined processing power of several mining computers dispersed over the globe is what powers cryptocurrencies.

Miners who are donating their computers for this purpose run these machines. They get paid or receive an incentive in exchange for their feedback. When miners figure out a complex mathematical puzzle and validate transactions before others do, they get paid.

A timestamp, a hash pointer, and transaction data are contained in every block of the blockchain.

Hashing Mechanism

In the context of cryptocurrencies, a hash function is an algorithm that, by definition, converts data of any size to a hash. Every block has a hash pointer, which always refers to the block before it. It serves as a pointer, which facilitates transaction tracking.

Evidence of Work

The majority of currently in-use blockchains operate on the Proof of Work principle. Simply put, the Proof of Work protocol or system is an economic measure that necessitates some labor on the part of the requesters. This job is frequently computer processing time. This lessens the likelihood of service misuse.

The first timestamping method developed for the blockchain is the Proof of Work technique. The most widely used proof-of-work algorithms are built on top of SHA-256 and Scrypt. Among cryptocurrencies, Scrypt is the most commonly utilized. SHA-3, Crypto-Night and Blake are some others.

GPU vs. CPU for mining

When it comes to mining cryptocurrencies, there are numerous choices. When cryptocurrencies first came out, you could efficiently use your computer to run the mining algorithms alone. Your home or office computer runs on a central processing unit (CPU) that is powerful enough to do mining tasks.

Initially, mining was as simple as downloading or gathering the necessary mining software and wallet for a coin of choice. After setting up the mining software to connect to their chosen cryptocurrency network, a miner would assign your machine to the cryptocurrency mining task.

Miners have shifted from CPU-based machines to GPU-based PCs in recent months and years. The graphics processing unit (GPU) on your computer is responsible for handling visual systems. In essence, a GPU is a CPU on steroids, with much greater power and task-specific functionality. Because of its specialization, the GPU is well-suited for jobs like mining cryptocurrencies.

CPU vs. GPU Capacity Comparison

A GPU can process 32—32-bit instructions in the same amount of time as a CPU core, which can only process four or 32-bit instructions per clock.

This merely indicates that 800 times more instructions are processed on each watch by a GPU processor.

A single GPU, such as the HD5970, is more than five times faster than four contemporary CPUs put together, even though the most recent models have up to 12 cores and far higher frequency clocks. As a result, GPU mining may lead to quicker transaction times and more significant coin gains over time.

Comparing the functions of the CPU and GPU

The CPU is the computer's executive branch. In essence, the central processing unit acts as a decision-maker under the guidance of the installed software. Arithmetic and logic units, or ALUs, are abundant on GPUs. Because of this, they are able to perform significantly more computational work in a larger volume than CPUs.

The fact that GPU mining has virtually rendered CPU mining obsolete is what should worry you. This is a result of the majority of bitcoin networks experiencing exponential growth in hash rate. Some Bitcoin networks hardly make money from CPU mining, while others are experiencing great success. It has been significantly impacted by the higher hash rate.

In contrast, GPU mining is substantially faster and, therefore, more profitable on all Bitcoin systems. GPU-based mining rigs are becoming increasingly crucial in bitcoin mining. A computer system or configuration used to mine currencies is called a mining rig. The majority of rigs are devoted to completing a single activity, in this case, mining cryptocurrency.

Section 4: The Digital Ecosystem

Exchanges for Cryptocurrencies: Doors to the World of Digital Currency

Exchanges are essential in the vast world of cryptocurrencies because they act as a link between conventional fiat money and the digital frontier. These marketplaces are necessary for both new and seasoned re about their importance, features, and factors to take into account while choosing one.

1. What Part Do Crypto Exchanges Play?

Fundamentally, a cryptocurrency exchange functions much like a stock exchange; only it deals with digital currencies rather than stocks. They function as:

Exchanges are the providers of liquidity, enabling consumers to buy or sell cryptocurrencies quickly.

2. Kinds of Exchanges for Cryptocurrencies

Centralized Exchanges (CEX): These are run by organizations that are centralized. They serve as middlemen, keeping users' money while offering a trading platform. Binance, Coinbase, and Kraken are a few examples.

Decentralized Exchanges (DEX): These online marketplaces enable peer-to-peer transactions devoid of a central body.

Exchanges that are hybrid: These exchanges combine elements of both DEX and CEX in an effort to provide the speed and liquidity of centralized exchanges with the security of decentralized ones.

User Interface: Professionals and novices alike can trade with ease thanks to a straightforward, easy-to-use interface.

Increased liquidity translates into quicker transaction times and more precise pricing.

Supported Coins: While some exchanges concentrate on the major coins, others help hundreds of coins. Depending on your trading requirements, this may be a crucial component.

Fees: Each exchange charges a certain amount for each transaction. To prevent unforeseen expenses, it is vital to comprehend these.

4. Points to Remember Regarding Exchange Regulatory Compliance Selection: Verify that the exchange abides by the laws of the nation in which it conducts business. This may provide an extra degree of security.

Reputation: Articles, news articles, and forum conversations regarding the importance of the exchange.

Geographical Restrictions: In some nations or areas, certain exchanges might not be available.

Customer service: For novice traders in particular, prompt and efficient customer service can be essential.

5. Cryptocurrency Exchanges' Future

Exchanges for cryptocurrencies have developed in tandem with the expansion of the cryptocurrency market. Businesses are likely to witness an influx of traditional financial instruments and products, such as futures, options, and perhaps ETFs, as legal frameworks become more apparent. Furthermore, as DeFi (Decentralized Finance) gains traction, decentralized exchanges will likely become even more critical to the ecosystem surrounding digital currencies.

6. Dangers and Obstacles

Exchanges carry some hazards even though they are essential in the world of cryptocurrencies.

Exchange Hacks: Throughout the years, a number of well-known exchange hacks have caused users to suffer significant losses.

Regulatory Crackdowns: Because of regulatory issues, a few exchanges have seen abrupt closures or limitations.

Price Manipulation: On smaller exchanges, price manipulation can occasionally result from low volume or liquidity.

The central nervous system of the digital currency market,

cryptocurrencyexchanges provide global users with liquidity, usability, and accessibility. These platforms will probably change as the cryptocurrency market grows, adding cutting-edge financial instruments, improving security measures, and providing a more comprehensive range of services. The first step to a successful crypto journey for anyone entering the world of digital currencies is knowing and choosing the correct exchange.

Investments And Wallets

What does the wallet look like? I understand that the wallet you carry in your pocket comes to mind, but this. We all own one of these, which is really impressive, and we use it to store our daily cash—not this wallet.

Allow me to present to you a novel kind of wallet. A wallet is a piece of software that interacts with different blog chains, saves private and public keys, and allows users to transfer Bitcoin between themselves and keep track of their total amount at any one time.

When sending cryptocurrency to another individual, for example, my friend has a wallet with a public key and a private key that he uses simultaneously. Thus, for that transaction to be completed when I deposit that cryptocurrency to him, both our public and private keys must match.

We call this a push mechanism. I'll come back to that later. Essentially, though, I forfeit possession of that portion of the Bitcoin once I complete that transaction. And he owns that piece as soon as it reaches his wallet.

Other than the leather wallet in your pocket, there are several kinds of audits. They are known as offline wallets or wallets. These are online wallets, sometimes referred to as hot wallets. These are genuine wallets. These are cellular wallets. These are wallets for desktop use. They have wallets and are online.

Depending on the kind of wallet you want to use, each of these has advantages and downsides. The exciting part is here: there are a few ways that Bitcoin investments might generate income for investors.

I will now use a term that you may need to become more familiar with total. If it's okay with you, I will explain it to you. Hodo is clinging on to the hope that Hodo will eventually invest in a cryptocurrency. Assume I invested in 21. Holding that cryptocurrency and waiting for it to travel from moon to moon would be equivalent to waiting for an exponential increase in price.

Thus, if I'm waiting for a price increase, I'm waiting for a 10 percent, 20 percent, or 30 percent increase. That will require a significant amount of time—a year, two, three, five, or ten years—to complete.

The idea behind this technique is to hold onto that coin for as long as possible because it keeps getting more and more valuable every year, month, etc. That coin can, therefore, continue to appreciate in value if I get rid of it the next month. And the month after that.

It's a long-range plan. Like everything else, it always pays to take your time, do your homework, and learn everything there is to know about a coin, including who creates it and how to use it, before investing money in it.

Understand the impact that coin can have on your life and the reasons for your desire to invest in it. The swing trade, which employs ideas we may have heard about before learning about day trading, is the second tactic.

Buy low, sell high, then. Over the years, you've heard a lot of people yelling that on the stock market: buy low, sell high. In swing trading, it is essentially what they do.

However, the margins are substantially lower when swing trading cryptocurrency.

Thus, the duration that we typically use is one or two days. Because cryptocurrencies are so volatile, they can increase by 10% one day and decrease by 10% the next.

Therefore, we're taking advantage of that volatility over a shorter time frame. When utilizing that method as opposed to, for instance, stocks or FX, those are subject to outside forces. Thus, both global macro events and global events can have an impact on them.

The rand or the dollar may weaken if the president is replaced. That's why those take longer than cryptocurrencies, which might fluctuate in value based on the status of the market or the sentiment of the public this week.

Again, a swing trade is primarily about using technical analysis to discover medium-term trends, so all of these methods require research.

Investing in an IPO is the third way that people can profit from cryptocurrencies.

An IPO: What is it? Might I ask? An initial coin offering is called an IPO. Thus, in a hypothetical scenario, let's assume I have a coin called AKG Quinn and I want investors to buy it in the beginning. And within that coin, I extend an early invitation for people to make an investment at a reduced rate with the expectation that it would increase in value over time.

This can be a hazardous method of making a profit because a coin could emerge one day and vanish the next, but it can also be a very successful one. As a result, you must thoroughly investigate everything the queen does.

Who is in charge of the coin, who created it, what it is used for, its name, etc. You have invested in that coin once more. You own the money. You have to be an expert on that coin. Consequently, the cryptocurrency lifespan.

While some cryptocurrencies have their unique lifecycle, most cryptocurrencies have a plottable lifecycle. I'm not claiming that this is how they will all turn out.

There is an initial phase known as the accumulation phase, which is essentially when cryptocurrency first gains traction, notoriety, and speed from people learning about its potential applications, whether or not it develops specific use cases, whether or not people are aware that they can use it for smart contracts, e-commerce websites, etc. It is the stage of accumulation. The mock up phase comes next.

A cryptocurrency can rise five, ten, or fifteen percent, and people will start to think, "Okay, I also want to be on this gravy train and I want to get as much out of this gravy train as possible." This is known as the mock up phase. This is usually when even the uninitiated investor begins to notice that a cryptocurrency is starting to gain pace and gain value.

Next, we reach the summit, the place where everyone aspires to be—the top of the iceberg or the meeting of the mountain. A coin can go from being nonexistent to having increased by 100% in worth, with the top of the cash receiving the most outstanding amount of value.

One hundred fifty-two hundred three hundred percent rise. That represents the pinnacle of cryptocurrencies. The distribution phase is when knowledgeable investors typically start selling off their currency because they are aware that it is beginning to decline. This decline may be caused by a variety of factors, such as people losing interest in and using the currency, a fork, the currency reducing from another coin, or something else entirely.

After it starts to decline, the contemporary period will begin. A currency enters the breakdown phase when it chooses to start depreciating significantly more. Thus, this is typically where the novice investor starts to get noticed.

If I'm a layperson, then that's when the money chooses to start running out on the cryptocurrency because I might still need to do my homework, know how to spot trends, or see when the markdown is approaching.

Because your return can be determined by where you enter and exit an investment, as is the case with any kind, you should conduct study and understand when to enter and exit the market. Purchase cheap. The investment principle is to sell high.

Can Cryptocurrency Be Successful?

In the present era, no word produces more confusion than cryptocurrency. The term is frequently used and seen by people, both in the media and even among friends and family. However, almost every time it is brought up, there are a lot of queries and outright mistrust. Over time, as bitcoin has grown in popularity, uncertainty has only deepened and gotten more challenging to overcome.

That's unfortunate because bitcoin is one of the most promising things of the twenty-first century. Those who have closely followed the cryptocurrency business have seen notable development, in fact. Naturally, there has been growth, but it needs to continue. Nobody will contest that. However, growth has been the key to many people's extraordinary financial success and stability. Additionally, it is the kind of potential that has drawn in novice investors as well as those who have never invested in a market before.

Furthermore, cryptocurrencies have caused a lot of disruptions. Above all, the world of cryptocurrencies has delivered a message to many people who have been involved in investing for a long time. The world, young and old alike, has seen that the status quo need not be the only way things are done thanks to cryptocurrency, which has delivered a shot across the bow and shook things up. Even after generations, items and objects can change.

More benefits have come from cryptocurrency than just the potential for massive financial gains. It has served as a means of demonstrating to the world the possibilities of modern technology and thought. Without a doubt, cryptocurrencies have been more than just assets traded on an utterly unrestricted market. It has been a message, a quiet protest that has made a significant impact nonetheless. Anyone who sees that needs to pay attention to the underlying principles and notion of cryptocurrencies.

A revolutionary and promising concept like cryptocurrency would have admirers everywhere. However, that is untrue. Individuals require assistance in comprehending it. Even the most knowledgeable and well-studied traders have fundamental inquiries. Yes, it is impossible to honestly describe what cryptocurrencies are, even for people who have spent decades studying Wall Street and making enormous profits through trading, buying, selling, and investing.

Numerous individuals, both in the professional and non-professional domains, require knowledge of cryptography, including its principles and operations. There is a great deal of confusion along with idle conjecture, gossip, and mistrust. Many people believe that cryptocurrencies are a hoax, a fraud, or a big swindle that would steal your money like a pyramid scheme. In fact, almost every belief regarding cryptocurrencies is firm and unwavering, despite the fact that many of the opinions are founded on false assumptions, ignorance, and lack of research.

Contrary to popular belief, cryptocurrencies aren't a shadowy fraud run by crooks hoping to exploit the internet to launder money or do other heinous crimes. There is no truth in that at all. For those who are willing to invest in the market, the truth is far more thrilling. In actuality, investing in cryptocurrencies is among the most excellent options available; it's a calculated move into a market that is still in its infancy and has to be fairly valued by a large number of people. Even if many people want assistance in accurately comprehending cryptocurrencies, this is acceptable for those who wish to profit. You stand to gain from that if your goal is to become a profitable and active cryptocurrency trader. Your power increases with your level of cryptocurrency understanding.

Your chances of making a lot of money increase the more you genuinely understand how it operates, why it operates, and how it might operate in the future.

Ten years ago, if you had asked experts whether it was wise to invest in virtual currencies, they would have laughed you off. Things have now improved. Unquestionably, cryptocurrency—a digitally encoded form of money—is the next big thing in the global financial system. With more than 5000 different kinds of cryptocurrencies in use, they will be around for a very long time and continue to grow.

When it comes to investments, cryptocurrencies are the most profitable asset class. Although cryptocurrency started out as a decentralized alternative to the traditional financial system powered by fiat money, it has rapidly supplanted other options as the preferred option for investors to store their cash. Cryptocurrencies with a positive reputation include

Ethereumand Bitcoin. A currency needs to be stable in order for its supply, usability, security measures, and acceptance to be in place. These factors can be used to determine whether bitcoin is a wise investment.

Yes, there is a lot of promise for cryptocurrencies. It is argued by some to have more significant potential than the majority of conventional forms of money. This is a result of its values, capabilities, and the infrastructure designed to support and safeguard it.

Indeed, one of the leading causes for people's belief in and investment in cryptocurrencies is its underlying technology. Like a well-oiled machine, that engine establishes and maintains checks and balances. And just like cryptocurrencies in general, that engine runs on and for the people. The individuals who use and support cryptocurrencies are also the ones that monitor them to make sure everything operates as it should.

A vital component of the cryptocurrency engine is a technology known as blockchain. Blockchain technology is, in certain respects, more intricate than cryptocurrencies. Blockchain is a vast system that functions like a live, breathing creature that never stops, and this fact cannot be disputed. Millions of moving parts make up this system. Nonetheless, the fundamental ideas and assumptions of blockchain are simple, much like cryptocurrencies. And it will open up trading, saving, and investment opportunities that can make you a small fortune once you fully understand them and understand how and why they operate.

However, blockchain is about much more than that, which is why its potential is so great. Blockchain is making its way into a wide range of businesses worldwide, including healthcare, automation, elections, shipping, and transportation. Blockchain is demonstrating its capabilities and how easily and effectively it can change entire industries. Blockchain has more potential than can be summed up because of this and many more factors. In the end, it has the ability to alter the course of events.

Things To Take Into Account While Choosing A Trading Bot

Strong security is essential for every online program, but cryptocurrency trading bots especially need it. You can wind up endangering yourself (and your money) if you use a bot developed by an unreliable company that has little to no online presence. This is because they have access to your money. It might be challenging to assess the security of cryptocurrency trading bots, but online forums and reviews can help you choose the best, safest choice.

dependable and dependable

Good cryptocurrency trading bots must be dependable because they must work around the clock and fulfill essential tasks when you need them most. You might miss a fantastic chance to lock in a profit, even if it's just for a short while, if you choose a bot that experiences connectivity issues.

Seek out as recent reviews as you can from other users. Use reviews or community sites to get a variety of viewpoints from genuine customers. A bot is more reliable the more happy people you can find.

Openness

Transparency is one of the main advantages of trading cryptocurrencies: since networks are open to the public, the likelihood of unethical activity and behavior is significantly reduced. The most secure, trustworthy, and well-known cryptocurrency trading bots employ a similar process.

Interface That's Easy to Use

Choose a bitcoin trading bot with an easy-to-use interface if you want the process to be as straightforward as possible. It is less likely that you will become confused with an uncomplicated design and short layout, which is particularly crucial when you are just getting started.

Turnover

If you're considering using bitcoin trading bots, research their profitability. If you're not getting a solid return on your investment, it's not worth using one. Take another look at what other people have to say.

Bots' Place in Cryptocurrency Trading

The values of cryptocurrencies are known to fluctuate significantly even in a matter of minutes. Additionally, investors can trade bitcoins at any time of day and from any location in the world. The efficacy of human bitcoin trading is severely restricted when these traits are combined.

First of all, a lot of investors can't respond to market changes fast enough to take advantage of the best deals that could be offered to them. Transaction delays and exchange lags make the issue worse. Secondly, investors need more time to devote to the cryptocurrency markets in order to place the most significant wagers consistently. This would need constant monitoring of bitcoin exchanges worldwide, seven days a week.

Thankfully, a lot of investors are able to resolve these problems.

Because they can respond faster than investors, bots have an advantage.

Most investors, however, lack the time to devote to always obtaining the most fantastic deal—something that bots can accomplish.

One important kind of bot is the arbitrage bot, which aims to profit from price differences between exchanges.

Bear Markets Are Not New

Bear markets are nothing new to Bitcoin users.

Similar to the Nasdaq in 2000, prices have dropped 45–50% throughout each negative wave in the current bear market. For many of the other cryptocurrencies that have been available for purchase for the last five years or so, bear markets are nothing new, and Bitcoin is not the first cryptocurrency to experience them.

The most well-known cryptocurrency available is Ethereum (ETH), which was introduced by computer programmer VitalikButerin in 2015. It sold for $0.311 when it first came on the market and reached $4,812 in August 2021, the highest value. In June 2022, Ethereum saw a decline below $1,000 for the first time since January 2021. For ETH, this was a 70% decline in the first half of 2022. A pattern akin to the previous cryptocurrency meltdown, in which Ethereum peaked in January 2018 at just under $1,400 before collapsing and trading around $112 in December of the same year (CoinMarketCap, 2022).

You have a unique second chance in the next 12 to 24 months if you missed the bear market of 2018–2020. You might decide to seize the opportunity wholeheartedly or to let another one pass through your fingers. For me, it's the latter.

Why am I saying this? In other words, cryptocurrencies gained more value in the bull market that succeeded the 2018–2020 crisis than they did in the bull run that preceded it. The biggest cryptocurrency in the world, Bitcoin, reached an all-time high of $68,990 in the final quarter of 2021, surpassing its previous record high of $19,783.03. As a result, in just four years, the value of the cryptocurrency increased by more than three times.

During this same time frame, other cryptocurrencies set new records besides Bitcoin. The various businesses and cryptocurrencies that made it through the 2018 crash delighted in varying degrees of success during the most recent bitcoin boom that followed the bull run. On the exchanges for the cryptocurrency market, Ethereum and several other new coins, including

Dogecoin, Solana, and Polkadot, all saw increases in value and new highs.

Several cryptocurrencies, including Stablecoins, which gave investors a chance to save money while being part of the cryptocurrency ecosystem, were also introduced during and after the 2018–2020 meltdown. Cryptocurrencies with the same value as fiat money, such as USD Coin (USDC) and Tether (USDT), were indexed to the US dollar.

It's not all bad news, either. Proficient investors generally agree that during the last four years, substantial returns have been made by individuals who entered the Bitcoin space during a slump. The market has a well-established cyclical nature; historical data shows that after a period of declining values, a bull run frequently follows, resulting in significant price appreciation. The current market offers the possibility of long-term financial gain, so now is a wise moment for you to expand your cryptocurrency investments.

Chapter 1: Overview of cryptocurrencies and blockchain technology

1.1 Digital money and blockchain technology

Cryptocurrencies are typically decentralized, which means they are not governed by a single central body or authority, in contrast to traditional currencies issued by central banks.

Under the pseudonym Satoshi Nakamoto, a person or group of persons established Bitcoin, the first cryptocurrency, in 2009. Thousands more cryptocurrencies have been developed since then, each with unique features, functions, and operating principles. Litecoin, Ethereum, Ripple (XRP), and Binance Coin (BNB) are a few of the most well-known.

Typically, blockchain technology—a distributed ledger—is the foundation of cryptocurrencies. Every transaction involving a cryptocurrency on a decentralized, open network is documented on the blockchain. A network of nodes, or computers connected to the blockchain, verifies each transaction.

A transaction is added to a block of transactions and added to the current blockchain once it has been validated. Cryptocurrency transactions may now be carried out swiftly, safely, and without requiring transaction verification from a reliable third party thanks to this technology[1].

Cryptocurrencies have been utilized as a investment in addition to being a payment method. This is due to the fact that cryptocurrencies are notorious for having sharp price swings that occur over brief periods. This implies that investors run the risk of both suffering significant losses and making large gains.

with order to avoid the costs and delays involved with conventional banking transactions, cryptocurrency users can also use them to send money internationally. They also provide a certain level of anonymity, which can be appealing to some individuals who want to carry out private transactions.

Even with their increasing appeal, cryptocurrencies are still a contentious and sometimes misunderstood subject. Because of their decentralization and ease of use for illegal operations like money laundering and financing terrorism, some regard them as a danger to the established financial system.

On the other hand, some regard cryptocurrencies as a significant technological breakthrough with potentially advantageous uses across various domains. The following are some possible advantages of blockchain technology and cryptocurrencies:

Anonymity: Users of cryptocurrencies can transact more discreetly and have their privacy protected, thanks to the relative obscurity that these technologies provide. Although this anonymity can be used illegally, it can also provide security against private invasions by other parties or government monitoring.

Financial democratization: Without a traditional bank account, people who are underbanked or unbanked can now access fundamental financial services thanks to cryptocurrencies. In places where access to banking services is limited, this can aid in the reduction of poverty and the promotion of financial inclusion.

Transparency: By logging every transaction on an unchangeable public ledger, blockchain technology promotes more openness. This can facilitate transaction verification for both individuals and corporations, lessen corruption, and enhance the traceability of cash.

Security: To safeguard transactions and prevent unwanted modifications to data, the blockchain employs sophisticated cryptography. This can lower the chance of fraud and hacking while fostering trust in online transactions.

Efficiency: By cutting out intermediaries and transaction costs, cryptocurrencies can enable quicker and less expensive payment methods. Delays and costs associated with overseas transfers can be significantly minimized by doing this.

Innovation Potential: Blockchain technology has the ability to revolutionize a number of industries, including healthcare, intellectual property, and supply chains. By making information more accessible and secure, it might, for instance, enhance product traceability, guarantee the accuracy of medical data, and safeguard intellectual property rights.

Decentralization: By decreasing reliance on conventional financial institutions and lowering the hazards connected with concentrated power,

Democracy and public participation: By enabling more accessible, safe, and transparent election procedures, blockchain technology can contribute to the advancement of democracy. Blockchain-based electronic voting systems ensure vote privacy and anonymity while reducing the possibility of fraud and tampering. Furthermore, using blockchain-based forums for debate and consultation, citizens can directly participate in decision-making and help formulate public policy. This is another way that technology can promote citizen involvement.

The collaborative economy and participatory finance can both be revolutionized by blockchain technology, which makes it possible for people and businesses to raise money in a decentralized, transparent, and safe way. Initial coin offers (ICOs) and security token offerings (STOs) are two examples of blockchain-based crowdfunding platforms that can facilitate capital access for companies and creative projects while offering investors a variety of funding options. Moreover, smart contracts can be used to guarantee transaction security and trust, allowing users to share goods and services on decentralized collaborative platforms without the need for intermediaries.

To sum up, blockchain technology and cryptocurrencies have enormous potential to change a lot of facets of our everyday lives as well as the world economy. Anonymity, financial democratization, transparency, efficiency, security, and innovation across multiple industries are some of the possible advantages. Furthermore, the decentralization of blockchain has the potential to revolutionize participatory finance and the collaborative economy while also enhancing democracy and citizen involvement. Even though there are obstacles and worries to take into account, these technologies have the potential to significantly alter civilization globally.

Beginner's Guide ToBitcoin Mining Software

Many people think that Bitcoin is the way of the future for trade, while some see it as just a fleeting fad. Although real money can be used to purchase Bitcoin, it is often "mined" using a combination of specialized hardware and software. If you're not sure what that means, don't worry—many beginners are. Although the word "mining" has historically been associated with gold and lost treasure, it can also refer to the process of obtaining digital cash.

The process of creating new cryptocurrencies and adding elements to an existing blockchain involves the usage of mining software for cryptocurrencies like Bitcoin. After it has been verified, the mining party adds the newly minted bitcoin to the Blockchain in exchange for a reward. Assuming that the ideal hardware and software combination can keep up with the system's stringent process, mining one bitcoin typically takes ten minutes. For individuals without access to a top-tier machine, mining a single coin can take up to thirty days.

These are a few of the most significant bitcoin mining software choices for novices.

1. DECEPTION

Qualities:

Every day, payments are paid.

Withdrawals have a shallow minimum of 0.001 BTC.

The minimum amount for a mining contract is $49

There is a helpful calculator for choosing a mining contract on the website (includes ordinary and pro versions)

Because of its incredible adaptability, CGMiner has been an essential participant. It is frequently regarded as the best bitcoin mining program on the market. It is C-based, open-source, and compatible with three different kinds of mining hardware: FPGA, ASIC, and GPU. It functions on Linux, Windows, and Macs. Aside from that, CGMiner offers additional benefits including better block identification, remote interface capabilities, and zero latency scaling to any hash rate.

4. ECOS ECOS is one of the leading cloud mining providers, having been established in 2017. Being the first company to operate in the Free Economic Zone legally, it offers cloud mining services. Approximately 90,000 individuals from all over the world use its services. In addition to providing mining services, ECOS is a fully functional investing platform. Its platform, which can be downloaded from Google Play or the App Store, also has a wallet, exchange, portfolios for investments, and savings.

5. BFGMinerBFGMiner was developed in 2012 by Luke Dashjr and enables users

to remotely control rigs, identify and start idle threads, and monitor hardware temperature. It has so succeeded in elevating itself to the top tier of mining software in terms of customization

BeMine has been operating in Russia and the CIS countries since the beginning of 2018. With more than 70,000Th/s in Irkutsk, Moscow, the Chelyabinsk region, Siberia, Almaty, and Kazakhstan, BeMine was among the first businesses to share ASIC-miners in the cloud. They never stop expanding. BeMine is a platform that unites miners and bitcoin enthusiasts from all over the world with Russian data centers.

7. SimpleMiner

EasyMiner is an open-source frontend for mining tools like CGMiner and BFGMiner that is based on a graphical user interface (GUI). The update lets you connect your bitcoin wallet and offers a more user-friendly interface. You can mine Litecoin, Bitcoin, and other cryptocurrencies using it as well, but you'll need an ASIC mining device and a Windows operating system.

8. SimpleMiner

For miners who choose not to use it, EasyMiner is an easy-to-use substitute for the widely used Command-Line Interface-based mining equipment. You can also get a graphical depiction of your data and results with this software, which can be very helpful. Those who wish to mine Bitcoin and Litecoin simultaneously can use this Bitcoin mining application. When EasyMiner is first launched, it automatically enters the "MoneyMaker" mode. This starts mining on a private pool using the CPU of your computer and creates a wallet for Litecoin for you.

9. BitMinterBitMiner is an open-source mining program with a graphical user interface, just like EasyMiner. It is compatible with nearly every central software platform, such as Linux, Mac OS X, and Windows. Additionally, it functions with mining equipment

including FPGAs, GPUs, and ASICs. You must sign up for BitMinter's mining pool, which has more than 450,000 members and is continually growing since 2001, in order to mine bitcoin with them. BitMinter intends to make Bitcoin mining and earning larger payouts easier for its customers, therefore before you can use the program, you must sign up for a mining pool.

10. Miner Kryptex

A patented Windows technology called Kryptex Miner can quickly identify the coin with the highest profit margin. It can perform complex distributed Bitcoin computations with ease. It is strongly suggested that newcomers start with this platform because of its user-friendly structure and clear instructions. Not to mention that you can manage mining with Kryptex from any location.

When you're just starting with bitcoin, it can be scary to put your money online.

I. Fundamentals of Trends

We all want to discover the key to successful trading as traders. The truth is that there isn't a foolproof formula, but trend trading is a crucial idea that helps to distinguish successful traders from unsuccessful ones.

Consider trends as the ocean's waves. Trend traders ride the waves of the marketplace, just like surfers do. However, it would help if you learned how to recognize a lock before you can ride one. This is when knowing the fundamentals of trends comes in handy.

We'll delve into the fascinating world of trend trading in this chapter and go over the key ideas you need to understand to be a profitable trend trader.

In this section, we'll discuss:

Finding Trends: To begin, let's clarify what a trend is and how it differs from noise and erratic price fluctuations. You will acquire the ability to recognize market patterns and differentiate between sideways, up, and down markets.

Methods of Trend Analysis: You'll discover various ways for spotting trends, such as market structure, trendlines, and levels of support and resistance. These are the key instruments for determining the momentum and direction of a movement.

Understanding Trend Strength: Trends can be strong or weak, and figuring out how strong a trend is will help you determine whether a trend reversal is likely. You will discover how momentum may be applied to trend trading and utilized to determine the strength of a trend.

Trading in the Long-Term Trend's Direction: Following the long-term trend is one of the cornerstones of trend trading. You will discover the significance of this as well as how to use various timeframes to recognize the long-term trend.

Consider trends as a roadmap that directs traders in the direction of their goals. The power of trend trading lies in its ability to identify the next big trend before anybody else and then ride it all the way to the top, making a sizable profit.

Trends: What Are They?

To succeed in the market as a trader, one must comprehend trends and know how to spot them. The overall direction of the market is represented by sensations, which can be either upward (bullish) or downward (bearish). It is crucial to understand that prices may also be ranging, or drifting sideways, rather than following a clear trend.

Positive, Bull Trends

Higher lows and highs are indicative of bullish trends. They signify a time when buyers are outnumbering sellers in the market, a sign of optimism and confidence. Prices are often rising during a bullish trend, and traders are searching for opportunities to purchase.

Essential characteristics of bull trends include:

With more tremendous highs and higher lows, prices are rising.

There are more buyers than sellers, which boosts market sentiment.

Traders are searching for chances to purchase since they believe that prices will keep growing.

What is a Bitcoin?

A buddy has told you excellent things about Bitcoin (BTC), and you have undoubtedly heard awful things about it on television. You may have already bought your first Bitcoins as well.

But the majority of people need to be more informed about Bitcoin, its purpose, and what it is. However, you are not to blame, my dear reader. The most disinformation that has ever been spread on a topic is most likely bitcoin. A generalist newspaper aims Bitcoin and the cryptocurrency market as a whole every day, every month, or every year. Furthermore, Bitcoin has reportedly died at least 1,000 times in the last few years, according to mainstream and generalist media.

What is Bitcoin, though? Bitcoin can be characterized as a peer-to-peer electronic money network. Bitcoin is a type of currency. Because of this, Bitcoin does not age or alter over time, despite what many media outlets say once a month.

When you hear someone discussing the worth of Bitcoin, they are talking about its monetary value. However, keep in mind that one Bitcoin will always be one Bitcoin since BTC is a kind of money whose value is constant. The dollar countervalue of Bitcoin fluctuates due to supply and demand. You are listening to someone who does not know about Bitcoin at all when they tell you that the cryptocurrency is dead because its short-term value relative to the US dollar is declining. Bitcoin doesn't age or change. Although its dollar countervalue could fluctuate, a bitcoin purchased five years ago still has the same value today. And Bitcoin will always exist as long as this is the case.

The goal behind the creation of Bitcoin was far higher and distinct from just financial speculation. Nobody invented Bitcoin with the intention of speculating with it. Rather than being a speculative instrument, Bitcoin was designed to be a brand-new, autonomous, decentralized medium of exchange. Bitcoin is a medium of exchange for money as well as a payment system.

Not all money has been regulated by governments, who set its circulation amount, inflation rate, and other features, as it does today. For instance, gold has been used as money for thousands of years and has never been regulated by a state. Gold was the preferred medium of exchange for money by humanity because it had many advantageous properties that made it ideal for that use, including:

Scarcity: The world's supply of gold is finite. There cannot be any more made. It keeps its worth as a result.

Durable: It is hard to destroy gold.

It's interesting to notice that contemporary money is neither durable (banknotes may be readily destroyed) nor scarce (a government can produce money at will).

Bitcoin is a symbol of the development of monetary systems in a modern society. Throughout human history, the means of exchange have frequently changed: from barter to gold to contemporary currencies, to mention a few. And it's getting ready to use Bitcoin, possibly.

Therefore, Bitcoin represents a significant advancement in the way that people utilize money. Governments and major financial institutions, who would lose direct control over money, would view it as a danger. A significant portion of the financial community and mainstream media consistently pronounce Bitcoin to be dead in the (futile) hope that more people will avoid it indefinitely.